AF598985

TECHNOLOGY THEN AND NOW
AIRPLANES
THEN AND NOW
CLARA MacCARALD
childsworld.com

Published by The Child's World®
800-599-READ · www.childsworld.com

Photography Credits
Photographs ©: Shutterstock Images, cover (background), cover (icon), 1 (background), 1 (icon), 3 (background), 3 (icon), 4, 5, 10, 18, 22; IM Photo/Shutterstock Images, cover (modern plane), 1 (modern plane); Rob Wilson/Shutterstock Images, cover (old plane), 1 (old plane); Kim Jihyun/Shutterstock Images, 7; John T. Daniels/Virginian-Pilot/AP Images, 9; Frank Peters/Shutterstock Images, 12–13; Anne Kitzman/Shutterstock Images, 15; Carolina K. Smith MD/Shutterstock Images, 17; Bony/Sipa/AP Images, 20

ISBN Information
9781503889491 (Reinforced Library Binding)
9781503891111 (Portable Document Format)
9781503892354 (Online Multi-user eBook)
9781503893597 (Electronic Publication)

LCCN 2023950313

Printed in the United States of America

Clara MacCarald is a freelance writer with a master's degree in ecology and natural resources. She lives with her family in an off-grid house nestled in the forests of central New York. When not parenting her daughter, she spends her time writing nonfiction books for kids.

TABLE OF CONTENTS

AIRPLANES

The first airplane flew in 1903. Since then, planes have changed a lot. People made airplanes bigger and faster. They built planes that could be used in wars. They made planes that could carry hundreds of people.

Now, planes fly around the world. Thousands of planes are in the sky every moment of the day. Billions of people fly in planes every year. They travel for vacation or business. Some visit family or friends.

People go to airports to fly in planes.

Planes are used to do many other things, too. Planes carry mail. They move fresh fruits and vegetables before those products go bad. Military planes are used to fight in wars. They can carry troops and supplies. Planes are used to study the weather. Planes are an important part of modern life.

TAKING FLIGHT

People have thought about flying since ancient times. In an ancient Greek story, a man named Daedalus (DED-uh-luss) made wings using feathers and wax. Leonardo da Vinci drew a flying machine in 1495. Its wings were supposed to flap.

In the 1800s, people got closer to creating planes that actually worked. George Cayley invented a new kind of wing. This wing did not move. It was curved to create **lift**. But Cayley did not have a way to power his flying machines.

People have built models of da Vinci's flying machine.

Instead, Cayley and others used curved wings to make **gliders**. One person flew by standing in the glider. Ropes connected the glider to a horse. The horse pulled the glider, and it rose into the air.

Other inventors made planes that had steam engines. One steam-powered plane hopped 165 feet (50 m) into the air. But this did not count as flying because the plane could not stay up. Then people started working on gas-powered engines. These engines were lighter and more powerful. In 1899, brothers Wilbur and Orville Wright started working on planes. They made their own engine. They also made **propellers**.

Orville Wright lay face down in order to fly the *Wright Flyer*.

In 1903, the Wright brothers took a plane called the *Wright Flyer* to a beach in Kitty Hawk, North Carolina. The *Wright Flyer* flew for 12 seconds. It was the first plane flight powered by an engine.

FORCES IN FLIGHT

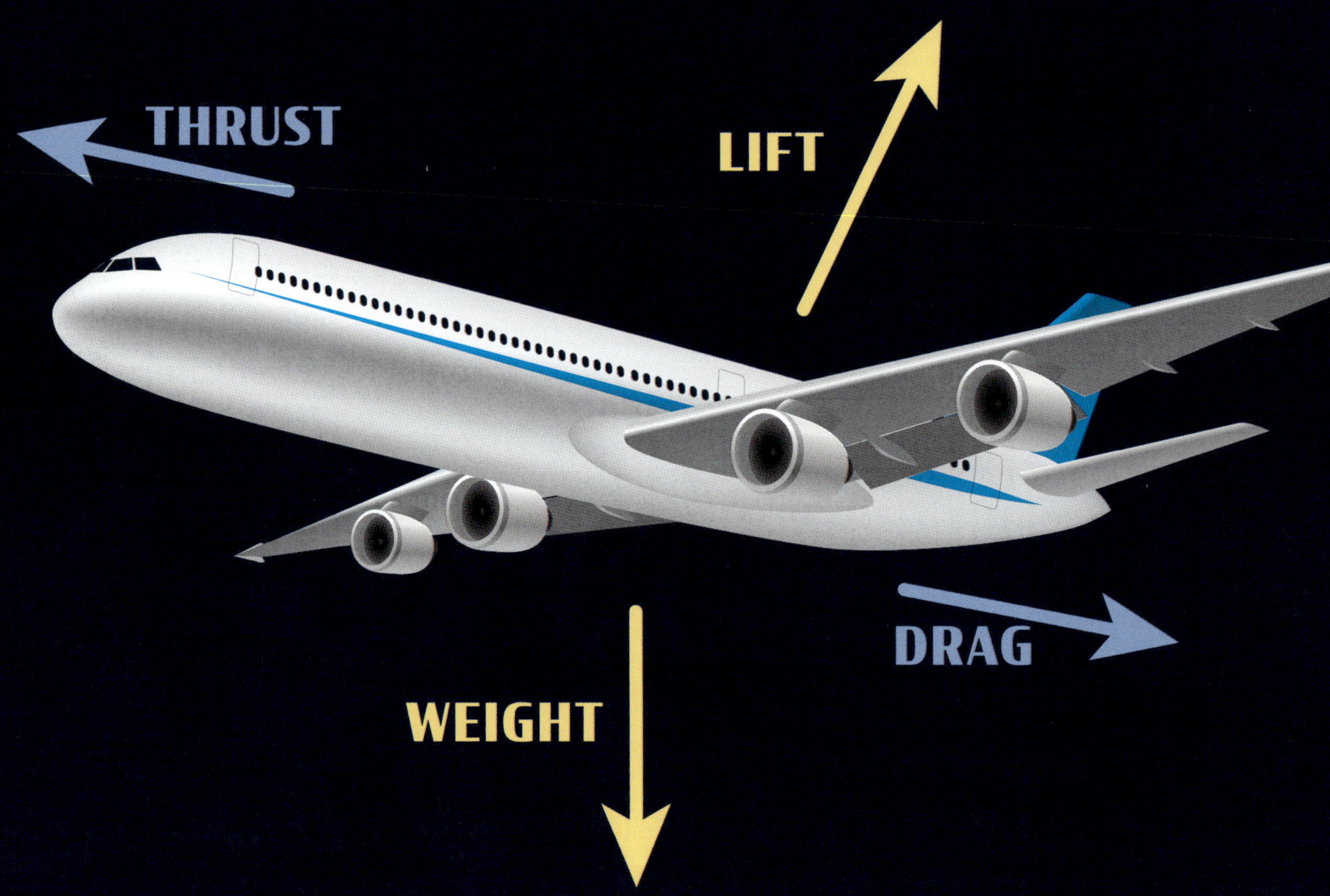

A plane in flight experiences four main forces. Lift pushes the plane up. Weight pulls it down. Thrust is the engine pushing the plane forward. Drag is the air pushing the plane back.

The Wright brothers and others continued to work on airplanes. Airplanes became larger and faster. They flew farther. Some planes started carrying **passengers**.

World War I (1914–1918) started. Airplanes became part of war. Militaries used planes to look for enemies. Planes dropped bombs. **Pilots** fought one another in the air.

Flying became more common for travelers after the war ended. People began building airports. Early flights were noisy and uncomfortable. Plane tickets were expensive. Still, some people were willing to pay a lot of money to travel in a plane.

CHAPTER 2

INTO THE JET AGE

In 1939, Germany attacked Poland. More than 1,000 German planes took part in the attack. World War II (1939–1945) began. Planes fought for control of skies around the world. The US military went from having about 2,500 planes before the war to having almost 300,000 by 1945.

The war led to new plane technology. Jet planes started out as military fighters. Jet planes power their engines with fast-flowing streams of gas or liquid. Jet engines replaced propellers on most planes. People started making larger and faster jet planes.

Jet engines are usually placed below an airplane's wings.

After the war, new wing and body shapes helped planes use less **fuel**. This allowed planes to fly farther. Wider planes had more seats for passengers. In the 1970s, air tickets became cheaper. More people could afford to fly. Many Americans who were not rich could now take vacations in places such as Europe.

New technology helped plan and direct flight paths. Instruments on the plane showed the pilot where to go. People on the ground began to use radio technology to find planes in the sky. These people could help guide a plane to safety in bad weather. Or they could keep planes from flying too close to one another. Satellites led to a new way of communicating with planes. Satellites are devices in space that **orbit** Earth. People use satellites to pass messages from the air to the ground and back.

MIDAIR REFUELING

Midair refueling is when one plane passes fuel to another through a hose as both aircraft fly. The first midair refueling happened in 1923. Militaries found midair refueling very useful. Planes didn't have to carry extra fuel or land as often.

People help guide planes from towers at airports.

AIRPLANES TODAY

Today, air travel continues to change. Many planes now have less space for each passenger in order to fit more seats. Planes show movies for passengers. Many flights offer access to the internet.

Planes have become safer. Officials pay more attention to things passengers bring on board. Officials scan bags and people for weapons. People have made planes that are better at withstanding bad weather. Planes can work in very hot or very cold temperatures. They can fly in heavy rain.

In the United States, people cannot take certain items on planes. These include weapons or things that could start fires.

Computer systems help pilots control a plane's speed and direction.

FLYING AND CLIMATE CHANGE

Planes put gases into the atmosphere. Those gases can add to climate change. Some people think that people should fly less to fight climate change.

Computers inside planes also make them safer. Some computers can spot if something on the plane is not working. People can fix that part before the plane flies again.

Many planes have a computer feature called autopilot. Autopilot can watch over the human pilot. It keeps the pilot from flying dangerously by accident. Autopilot can also fly the plane by itself. Pilots often have autopilot take over when flying long distances.

People are working on new plane technology, such as augmented reality (AR). AR displays pictures or words from a computer over a view of the real world. People who check planes for problems wear special glasses. The glasses use AR to help the people understand what they are looking at on the plane.

The Velis Electro is powered by electricity. It was first made in 2020.

People have invented electric planes. Electric planes could cause less **pollution** than fuel planes. Electric planes cannot carry many passengers. They cannot go very far. But someday they might. There is a lot to look forward to in the future of plane technology.

WONDER MORE

Wondering about New Information

How much did you know about airplanes before reading this book? What new information did you learn? Write down three new facts that this book taught you. Was the new information surprising? Why or why not?

Wondering How It Matters

What is one way that airplanes relate to your life? If you cannot think of a personal connection, imagine a way that airplanes might affect other kids. What impact might airplanes have on their lives?

Wondering Why

People created planes that could go farther and carry more weight using less fuel. Why do you think it is important for planes to use less fuel? Do you think this benefits the world as a whole?

Ways to Keep Wondering

The history of airplanes is a complex topic. After reading this book, what questions do you have about it? What can you do to learn more about airplanes?

FAST FACTS

- In 1903, the Wright brothers flew in the first airplane that was powered by an engine.
- Planes were used to fight in World War I and World War II.
- At first, few people could afford to fly.
- Jet planes use streams of gas or liquid to power their engines.
- In the mid to late 1900s, people made bigger and faster planes.
- In the 1970s, plane tickets got cheaper, and more people began to fly.
- Planes today have computers that make them safer. The autopilot feature can even fly a plane by itself.
- People are working on new plane technology, such as electric planes. Electric planes cannot carry many passengers or fly very far, but they might be able to in the future.

GLOSSARY

climate change (KLY-mit CHAYNJ) Climate change is the warming of Earth and changing of weather caused by human activities. Flying is one human activity that is adding to climate change.

fuel (FYOO-uhl) Fuel is something used to make energy. Planes use a lot of fuel to travel.

gliders (GLY-durs) Gliders are objects that fly without an engine. People invented gliders before airplanes.

lift (LIFT) Lift is a force that pushes up. Planes stay in the sky because of lift.

orbit (OR-bit) To orbit something is to circle around it in space. Satellites orbit Earth.

passengers (PAS-uhn-jurs) Passengers are people traveling in a plane. Bigger planes can carry more passengers.

pilots (PY-luhtz) Pilots are people who fly planes. Pilots must learn a lot about planes in order to fly safely.

pollution (puh-LOO-shuhn) Pollution is something harmful added to the environment. Planes add pollution to the air by burning fuel.

propellers (pruh-PEL-urs) Propellers are blades that turn to make force in order to move an object. Early planes flew with propellers.

FIND OUT MORE

In the Library

Henzel, Cynthia Kennedy. *Powerful Military Aircraft.* Parker, CO: The Child's World, 2024.

Higgins, Nadia. *Transportation Then and Now.* Minneapolis, MN: Jump!, 2019.

Jenner, Caryn. *First Flight: The Story of the Wright Brothers.* New York, NY: DK Publishing, 2023.

On the Web

Visit our website for links about airplanes:
childsworld.com/links

Note to Parents, Caregivers, Teachers, and Librarians: We routinely verify our web links to make sure they are safe and active sites. So encourage your readers to check them out!

INDEX